The Child's World

Published by The Child's World®
1980 Lookout Drive • Mankato, MN 56003-1705
800-599-READ • www.childsworld.com

ACKNOWLEDGMENTS
The Child's World®: Mary Berendes, Publishing Director
The Design Lab: Design and page production
Red Line Editorial: Editorial direction

LIBRARY OF CONGRESS CATALOGING-IN-PUBLICATION DATA
Heinrichs, Ann.
  Nouns / by Ann Heinrichs ; illustrated by Dan McGeehan and David
Moore.
    p. cm.
  Includes bibliographical references and index.
  ISBN 978-1-60253-429-2 (library bound : alk. paper)
  1. English language—Noun—Juvenile literature. I. McGeehan, Dan, ill.
II. Moore, David, ill. III. Title.
  PE1201.H373 2010
  428.2—dc22   2010011459

Printed in the United States of America in Mankato, Minnesota.
July 2010
F11538

ABOUT THE AUTHOR

Ann Heinrichs was lucky. Every year from grade three through grade eight, she had a big, fat grammar textbook and a grammar workbook. She feels that this prepared her for life. She is now the author of more than 100 books for children and young adults. She has also enjoyed successful careers as a children's book editor and an advertising copywriter. Ann grew up in Fort Smith, Arkansas, and lives in Chicago, Illinois.

ABOUT THE ILLUSTRATORS

Dan McGeehan spent his younger years as an actor, author, playwright, cartoonist, editor, and even as a casket maker. Now he spends his days drawing little monsters!

David Moore is an illustration instructor at a university who loves painting and flying airplanes. Watching his youngest daughter draw inspires David to illustrate children's books.

Milk!

TABLE OF CONTENTS

What Is a Noun?

All the words above are **nouns**. They name people, places, or things.

People	Places	Things
Claire	Connecticut	cat
Chris		cookies
		crayon
		corn

Most nouns start with **lowercase letters**.

The dog chased the frog off the log.

Proper nouns start with **capital letters**. These nouns are the names of certain people, places, or things.

My dog Lady likes to play.

I go to Taylor Elementary School.

If you say school, you can mean just any school. But Taylor Elementary School is an official name. That's why each word of this proper noun starts with a capital letter. Claire, Chris, and Connecticut are proper nouns too!

7

One or More?

monster lunch apple

A noun is **singular** if it names just one thing.

monsters lunches apples

A noun is **plural** if it names more than one thing.

How do you make a noun plural? You usually add an *s* or *es* at the end.

monster + s = monsters
lunch + es = lunches

Watch Out for Y!

monkey   baby   toy   penny

Watch out for nouns that end in the letter *y*. Some of these nouns use *s* to become plural, but some don't. How can you tell which way to go?

I saw six monkeys.

They were playing with toys.

Look at the letter before the *y*. If it is a vowel, just add *s* to the end of the word. The vowels are *a*, *e*, *i*, *o*, and *u*.

The babies cry a lot.

I found three pennies.

In baby and penny, the letter before the *y* is not a vowel. Take away the *y* and add *ies* to make them plural.

Step one: baby – y = bab

Step two: bab + ies = babies

I want toys and candies!

Tricky Plurals

What happens when one child is jumping rope and another joins in? You don't say two "childs" are playing. You say two children. There's no song about three blind "mouses." It's three blind mice!

Some nouns don't use *s* to become plural. You already know a lot of these tricky plurals.

Foot becomes feet.
Goose becomes geese.
Man becomes men.
Leaf becomes leaves.

One Moose, Three Moose

Some nouns stay the same whether they are singular or plural.

What if a moose walked into your kitchen? You might say, "Oh dear, there's a moose in here!" Suppose two more clomped in. You might shout, "Get these moose out of my house!"

The word moose stays the same, no matter how many there are.

Most nouns that don't change form are animal names. Examples are:

deer   sheep   moose   elk   trout

Mom, the moose is drinking the milk again.

Pull Up Your Pants!

Some nouns are always plural.

Would you ever pull up just one "pant"? Of course not! The word is always pants. The same goes for scissors, clothes, and shorts.

Please pass me the scissors.

What clothes should I wear today?

How Much Rice?

Some nouns never become plural. You can't get stuck in two traffics. You can't breathe in six airs.

These are things you do not count. Many such nouns are foods or drinks.

juice   milk   rice   cheese   butter

You might have three glasses of juice or two bowls of rice—but not three juices or two rices.

19

A Gaggle of Geese

Some groups have their own names.

A group of birds fly in a flock. Sheep stick together in a flock, too. Elephants, cows, and deer hang out in herds, while geese gather in a gaggle. Wolves roam around in a pack, and fish swim in a school.

Some groups of people have names, too.

family   crowd   class

Two Nouns Team Up

Compound nouns are made from two or more words put together.

Join *base* and *ball*, and what do you have? Baseball, of course! It's an easy way to say "a ball game with bases." Can you think of other nouns that are made from two words?

A pot that holds tea is a teapot.

How to Learn More

AT THE LIBRARY

Cleary, Brian P. *A Lime, a Mime, a Pool of Slime: More about Nouns.* Minneapolis, MN: Carolrhoda, 2008.

Cleary, Brian P. *A Mink, a Fink, a Skating Rink: What Is a Noun?* Minneapolis, MN: Carolrhoda, 1999.

Fisher, Doris. *Touchdown Nouns.* Pleasantville, NY: Gareth Stevens, 2007.

McClarnon, Marciann. *Painless Junior Grammar.* Hauppauge, NY: Barron's Educational Series, 2007.

Reeg, Cynthia. *Hamster Holidays: Noun and Adjective Adventures.* St. Louis, MO: Guardian Publishing, 2009.

Schoolhouse Rock: Grammar Classroom Edition. Dir. Tom Warburton. Interactive DVD. Walt Disney, 2007.

ON THE WEB

Visit our home page for lots of links about grammar: *childsworld.com/links*

NOTE TO PARENTS, TEACHERS AND LIBRARIANS: We routinely check our Web links to make sure they're safe, active sites—so encourage your readers to check them out!

Glossary

capital letters (KAP-uh-tul LET-urs): Letters including *A*, *B*, *C*, and so on used at the beginning of a sentence. Proper nouns begin with capital letters.

compound nouns (KOM-pound NOUNS): Nouns that are made up of at least two words. *Baseball* and *teapot* are compound nouns.

lowercase letters (loh-er-KASSE LET-urs): Letters including *a*, *b*, *c*, and so on used throughout a sentence. Nouns that are not proper nouns begin with lowercase letters.

nouns (NOUNS): Words that name people, places, and things. *Claire*, *Connecticut*, and *cookie* are nouns.

plural (PLOOR-uhl): A noun is plural if it names more than one thing. *Monsters* and *cookies* are plural nouns.

proper nouns (PROP-ur NOUNS): Nouns that name specific things or official things. People's names, such as *Claire* or *Chris*, are proper nouns.

singular (SING-gyuh-lur): A noun is singular if it names one thing. *Monster* and *cookie* are singular nouns.

Index